HELLO GOD

**A book of prayers
for young children**

compiled by
ALISON WINN

Illustrated by Diane Matthes

Henry E. Walter Ltd
Worthing, Sussex

Warner Press, Inc.
Anderson, Indiana

This is my own book of verse and of prayer.
It's about living, and learning to share
Your wonderful love, which is everywhere.

Here in my book, there are prayers I can say,
For things that are happening every day.

I can read it,

and write in it,

draw in it, too.

Paste a photograph of yourself in this space.

Hello, God, it's . . . . talking to you.

I have called you by your name, and you are my own.

Isaiah 43:1

The Family of God

Some families are very big
Some families are small.
Some people have no family
No family at all
But they, like everyone can be
Part of God's loving family.
And every one of us can share
The comfort of his loving care.

Dear God, be with us all wherever we are,
Near or far.
For every one of us is part of
Your great family.

Please, God, give your blessing to
Each and every one of us.
Help us to be unselfish and
Thoughtful for one another.

God who made the grass
The flower, the fruit, the tree,
The day and night to pass,
careth for me.

We love because God first loved us.

1 John 4:19

Prayer

P rayer is
Talking to God,
Listening to God,
Loving God.

G od, be in my head and in my understanding
God, be in my eyes and in my looking
God, be in my mouth and in my speaking
God, be in my heart and in my thinking
God, be at my end and at my departing.

From The Book of the Hours (1514)

J esus loved the children
Children just like me.
Often he would call them to gather round his knee
Patiently he'd listen to what they had to say
Tell them wonderful stories
And teach them how to pray.

L ord of the loving heart
May I be loving, too;
Lord of the gentle hands,
May mine be gentle, too;
Lord of the willing feet
May mine be willing, too;
So that I may daily grow
A little more like you.

Every good gift, every perfect gift, comes from above.

James 1:17

The Lord's Prayer

O ur Father
Who art in heaven,
Hallowed be thy name;
Thy kingdom come;
Thy will be done;
On earth as it is in heaven.
Give us this day our daily bread,
And forgive us our trespasses,
As we forgive those who trespass against us
And lead us not into temptation;
But deliver us from evil.
For thine is the kingdom, the power
And the glory, for ever and ever.
Amen.

Pictures of my Family and Friends

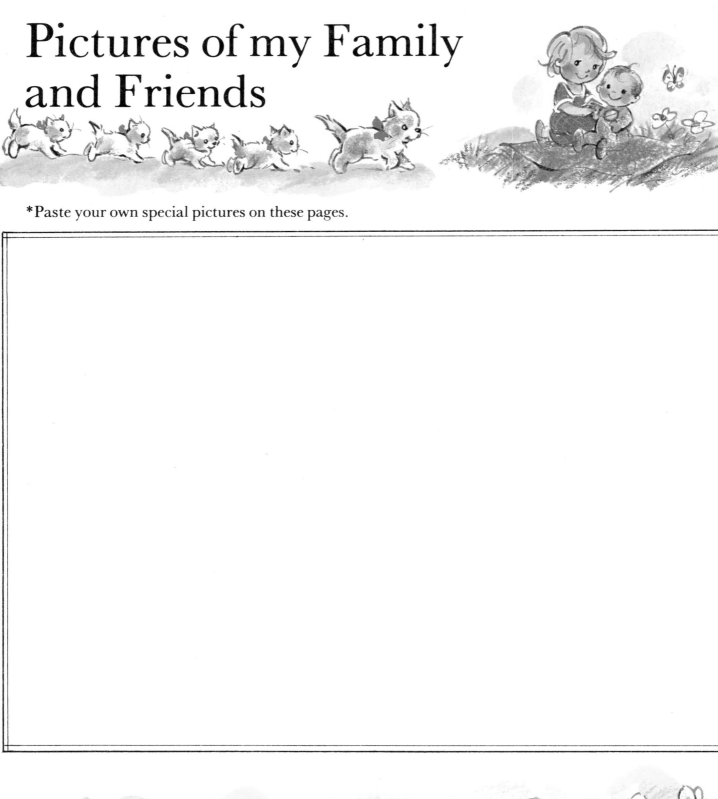

*Paste your own special pictures on these pages.

Good Morning!

God's mercies are new every morning.
Lamentations 3:23

Hello, God, here's another day
With friends to meet and games to play
Things to do, and books to read
The food, the comfort that we need.
May I always grateful be
For all that you have given to me.

Today I shall do a number of things
like running and racing and swinging on swings
And laughing and playing and learning to be,
Healthy and happy and closer to thee.

Dear Lord Jesus, we shall have this day only once;
before it is gone, help us to do the good
we can, so that today is not a wasted day.

(From a prayer by Stephen Grellett, 1773–1855)

Dear Jesus, we are free to choose
The thoughts we think, the words we use
But children can forgetful be, help me
To pray more thoughtfully.

Morning has broken like the first morning
Blackbirds have spoken like the first bird.
Praise for the singing! praise for the morning!
Praise for them springing, fresh from the word!

Eleanor Farjeon

Day by day, dear Lord, of thee
Three things I pray
To see thee more clearly
Love thee more dearly
Follow thee more nearly
Day by day.

Richard of Chichester (1197–1253)

Make me, Lord, polite and kind
to everyone, I pray;
And may I ask you how you find
Yourself, dear Lord, today.

John Bannister Tabb

Graces

Give thanks to the Lord for he is good.

Psalm 118:1

For each refreshing drink
For every tasty plateful
Let us pause to think
We should be truly grateful.

Thank you, heavenly Father, for clothes to wear
For food to eat, and your loving care
Which is all around us everywhere.

Dear Lord, I'm sure we ought'er
Thank you for giving us water,
Without which, I've no doubt,
We could not do without.

As our daily meals appear
Every day throughout the year
May we ask you, Lord, to bless
Those who grow the food for us.

Thank you for the world so sweet
Thank you for the food we eat
Thank you for the birds that sing
Thank you, God, for everything.

All good gifts around us
Are sent from heaven above.
Then thank the Lord, O thank the Lord
For all his love.

Whenever I sit down to eat
Dear Lord, I must think of the needy,
and not gobble up like a gannet,
A bird who is remarkably greedy.

Thank you, God, for our good food
And for those who prepare it.
Thank you for the table, too
Where families meet to share it.

God is great, God is good
Thank you for our daily food.

Wherever, whenever we meet to eat
Let us give thanks, dear Lord.

Come, dear Jesus, be our guest, and
Bless what you have given to us.

For food to eat, and those who prepare it
For health to enjoy it, and friends to share it
We thank you, O Lord.

Charles Shepherd

Each time we eat, may we remember God's love.
(A prayer from China)

People, Places, Playthings, Pets

On these pages stick any picture that
you like and want to keep.

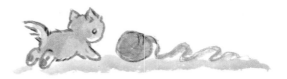

Prayers, for my Home, my Family, my Friends

A friend loves at all times.
Proverbs 17:17

A friend is a wonderful thing to have,
And a wonderful thing to be.
Talking, and playing, being together
Having each other to tea.
How lucky I am to have .... for a friend
I hope .... likes having me.

Help me, God, to show how much
I love my parents by
helping them in any way I can.
Like me, sometimes they get very
tired at the end of the day, so please
help me to remember to clear up my
toys before I go to bed.

God who gives all things to me
Thank you for my family.
Grandpa's very special way
Of listening to the things I say.
Grandma, too, who cheerfully makes
Gloves and toys and birthday cakes
And both who happily agree
That I love them, and they love me.

Bless this house which is our home
May we welcome all who come.

Thank you, God
For wild days
For wet days
For windy days
Cold and freezing toe days
Icicles on nose days.
Being out on those days
Makes it *so nice* coming in.

Thank you, dear God, for the welcome
and comfort of my home on winter days.

Bless my friends, Lord, and their friends,
And all their families too.
May they share the happiness,
That comes from loving you.

Birthdays

Every day is someone's birthday, Lord.
Today I am thinking of ....
Help me to make it a very special day
In every possible kind of way.
And may your ever-loving care
Keep .... safe throughout the year.

BIRTHDAY NIGHT

Tomorrow is my birthday, Lord.
  As year by year I grow;
Help me to see more clearly, Lord,
The way that I should go.
Learning to love
Learning to live
Learning to use the gifts I have.
Tomorrow is my birthday, Lord,
And I'll be one year older.

Help us, Lord, to be thankful for the gifts we have
received and to share with others who are in need.

My heavenly Father, all last year you took care of me,
  And now you have given me a birthday.
I thank you for all your goodness and kindness to me.
You have given me loving parents, a home, gifts and clothes.
Help me to be a better child in the coming year...
To grow strong, to study well and to work happily.

(A prayer from Japan)

Pictures to keep

On these pages stick any picture that you like and want to keep.

Thinking about other People

Help carry one another's burdens.

Galatians 6:2

Today my prayers, dear Lord,
  Are for the hungry people.
For fathers who can't find work to do
For mothers who have no money to buy food
For children who are sick and frightened
And old people who are frail and lonely.
Show me, dear Lord, how I can help in some small way.

Today I am thinking about the children who can't run
  and dance and play like me. Some who can't speak or hear
or see. Please be close to them, dear Lord, and take care
of the patient people who take care of these children.

Thank you, dear Lord, for a happy day.
  Tonight in my prayers I want to say:
Bless all little children wherever they be
Who haven't a home, or a bed like me.
And specially, Lord, I ask you please
To comfort the homeless refugees.

NIGHT WORKERS

I'm thinking of the engine drivers,
  Driving through the night.
Policemen on their lonely beat,
Firemen with fires to fight.
Doctors, nurses, factory workers.
Be with them, dear Lord,
While most of us are sleeping,
They are working hard.

Dear Lord Jesus,
Be with the doctors and nurses and everyone who brings help and comfort to people who are ill. May your strength be with them so that they do not get *too* tired.

If the postman has parcels he rings or knocks
Letters or postcards he pops in the box.
The postman's my friend, and a friend of mine
Is the boy with the papers who comes before nine.
There's that man with a book who reads the meter,
The coalman, the milkman, the window cleaner.
They're all busy people who work hard all day
So bless them, dear Lord, as they go on their way.

Thank you, God, for the people who
keep our school clean and tidy,
and for the people who cook our dinner.

The world is full of most interesting people.
I guess someone brave must have built that steeple.
Who was it I wonder put swings in the park,
And fixed rows of lights to shine out in the dark?
Someone built tunnels and bridges and highways,
Ships for the ocean, planes for the skyways.
There's so much to look at and so much to see,
Invented by people once little like me.

Thinking about Animals and Birds

The earth is full of your creatures
Psalm 104:24

Thank you, dear Lord, for my animal friends,
Guinea pigs, gerbils and rabbits,
Tortoises, white mice, cats and dogs,
All who have lovable habits.
Help me to care for them,
Feed them and water them,
Treat them with kindness, much I can learn from *them*.
They cannot speak, but they *do* understand
The sound of a voice and the touch of a hand.

If I'm allowed to keep a pet
Make sure, dear Lord, I don't forget
That he is mine. I must not let
The poor thing be neglected.

Oh heavenly Father, protect and bless
all things that breathe. Guard them from evil
and let them sleep in peace.

Albert Schweitzer

A little brown bird looked in to see
What I was having on bread for tea
He looked so hungry I felt I must
Eat the middle and leave him the crust.

The very next day he came again
Shivering cold in the pouring rain
'I'm hungrier *still* today,' he said
So I ate the crust and gave him the bread.

Now every day, whatever the weather,
That sparrow and I have our tea time together
We chirrup and chatter like very old friends
And I eat the odds up, while he eats the ends.

Every day I learn something new
To dress myself, to fasten my shoe
To care for my kitten, to tidy my room.
Reading and writing I'm going to learn soon.
But with all of these new things I'm trying to do
I promise, dear Jesus, I'll not forget you.

My School

Whatever you do,
work at it with all your heart.

Colossians 3:23

Thank you for the books we borrow
and for the stories our teachers read.

Dear Lord,
If sometimes we think other children are stupid,
we mustn't laugh at them. Help me to understand
that they may know lots of things that *we* don't know.

Dear God,
Help me to be kind and helpful to the children
in my school who come from other lands. Some
are having to learn new words and new ways of
doing things which must seem strange and
difficult. I'm sure we should find things
very different if we had to live in any other country.

Thank you for the new friends we make at school,
for the fun of walking home together and
sharing our secrets.

Heavenly Father,
Thank you for our school.
For singing and dancing and playtime with our friends.
For the letters and words we learn to write
For the numbers we count, and the pictures we draw.
And for all the interesting things we do with our hands.

Spring

For God so
loved the world.

John 3:16

A long time ago I planted a bulb
in my own little garden bed.
I buried it deep in the dark cold earth;
It was shrivelled and looked quite dead.
I waited and watched through the winter days
Till my fingers and toes grew quite chilly;
Then one day it happened, my little brown bulb
Burst into a gold daffo-dilly.

Fluffy chickens, soft and yellow,
Primroses and pussy willow
Frisky lambs with wobbly legs,
Hot cross buns and Easter eggs.
Oh, how happy I should be
Jesus lives, and he loves me.

Easter is a joyful time
The risen Jesus lives
And we know we will fulfil
All his promises.
Jesus who died for me
Help me to live for thee
So I may joyful be
Sure of your love.

For the flowers that bloom about our feet
For tender grass so fresh and sweet
For song of bird and hum of bee
For all things fair we hear and see
Father in heaven our thanks to thee
Who made our wonderful world.

Dear God,
Thank you for the spring when the whole world
comes to life and everything is fresh and green and
beautiful. Help us to look and listen, and enjoy
your wonderful world.

Summer

Thank you, God, for holidays,
  picnic places, jolly days
Miles of country, miles of sea,
Rock pools cool and shimmery
Where small slippery treasures hide
Washed in by the morning tide.
Limp green seaweed, tiny crabs,
jellyfish and baby dabs.
Shrimps and shells and pebbles small
And, dear Lord, you made them all.

Thank you, God, for summer days
  For the warmth of the sun, and busy buzzing of the bees.
And for just being alive.

The world is full of a number of things
  I'm sure we should all be happy as kings.

Thank you for the summer showers
  That freshen up the drooping flowers.
Thank you too for happy hours
Playing out of doors.

Autumn

The whole earth is full
of God's glory.

Isaiah 6:3

Thousands of tiny ears of wheat
   Make the tasty bread we eat.
Thousands of bees fly miles, it's said
To gather the honey we spread on bread.
Tons of apples and pears and cherries,
Nuts from the hedges and big blackberries,
Cabbages, cauliflowers, beans and peas,
How blessed we are to have all of these.
Yes, all this food, and much, much more
Come from God's wonderful bountiful store.

Thank you, dear Lord, that once again
   The barns are full of golden grain
The fruit trees are laden
The store houses full
The cows give us milk
And the sheep give us wool,
For which we are all truly thankful.

The corn sheaves are gathered, the apples are red
   The leaves from the trees are crumpled and dead
The mornings are misty, the brown starlings sing
We've planted the tulips to flower in the spring.

Now all the trees stand dark and bare
   And everywhere there is a carpet of gold.
And oh what fun it is to go stomping
Through the fallen leaves in my big winter boots
And to smell the smoky smell of autumn.
Thank you, God, for autumn days.

The golden sunshine, gentle air
   Sweet flowers and fruit your love declare
When harvest ripens you are there
Your many blessings with us to share.

Winter

THE NEWBORN KING

The Christ child lay
On his bed of hay
And a thousand stars looked down
And the angels sang of peace and joy
For the Holy Child,
For the baby boy,
For the king without a crown.

Little Jesus, sweetly sleep, do not stir
We will lend a coat of fur.
We will rock you, rock you, rock you,
We will rock you, rock you, rock you:
See, the fur to keep you warm
Snugly round your tiny form.

In winter it snows
And my fingers and toes
Are tingling and cold as can be.
There is ice on the lake
And enough snow to make
A snowman much bigger than me.

Something happened in the night
Silent, without sound
Sweeping, swirling snowflakes fell
Softly to the ground.

Something happened in the night
How wonderful to wake
And see the whole world sugar white
Like icing on a cake.

Thank you, God, for the winter snow
that makes the world so beautiful.

Dear God
Thank you for the joy of Christmas,
When families gather together.
When gifts are given and carols are sung.
And we think of the baby Jesus.

When Jesus was a growing boy
He learned his father's trade.
For Joseph was a carpenter
And useful things he made
Like boats and benches, chests and stools.
Joseph was clever with his tools.
I guess young Jesus longed to be
A carpenter as good as he.

He must have found it difficult
To chisel, saw and plane.
I guess he sometimes spoiled the wood
And had to start again.
Until he'd tried, and tried, and tried
I doubt if he'd be satisfied.
But, oh, he must have found it good
While cutting, shaping, smoothing wood.

Take my hands and let them move
at the impulse of your love.

My own Prayers

Write or paste in your own prayers on this page.

Help me to be unselfish, Lord, with
my books, my toys, my sweets.
Sometimes I find it hard to share
my things with other people.
But when I do it makes me happy.

Help me, dear Lord, when I wake
Up in the dark and feel afraid.
May I remember night and day
You are close beside me.

Some days I wake up feeling like a great black cloud.
Nothing seems right and I don't love anybody.
On those days I need you more than ever, dear Lord.
Please let the sunshine of your grace
take the frown off my face.

Help me to remember to say *please* and
thank you. Little words that mean so
much, but are often forgotten.

Help me, dear Lord, to make friends
by being friendly.
Someone has to say 'Hello' first, so
why not me?

By and by all things must die
We know this is so.
Animals, birds, the flowers, the trees
People we love, whose lives we share
This is the hardest loss to bear.
When we are sad, Lord, you are there,
Loving and understanding.

Playtime is fun, running, skipping,
jumping and playing all sorts of
jolly games with our friends.
When you were a child, Lord Jesus,
I'm sure you enjoyed playtime, too.

Help me, Lord, to remember you in the good times,
not just to call on you when things go wrong.

When I am unhappy, Lord, help
me to share my troubles with you.
You'll understand why I am crying,
and that will be comforting to know.

Lord, I am sailing on your wide, wide sea
Please guard my little ship for me.

God's Wonderful World

Sing for joy to the Lord, all the world.

Psalm 100:1

THE CHERRY TREE

Sitting up here on the cherry tree,
A lot of God's wonderful world I see
A lot of God's interesting people too,
Busily doing what people do.
Over the fence clean laundry is blowing
Next door a man is digging and hoeing.
They're sizzling something across the way
A barbecue must be planned for today.
Further away in a field of clover,
Playful puppies roll over and over.
When I climb higher I really can see,
The church in a square, and the chestnut tree.
There are trucks, cars and buses rushing about,
While people pop into the shops or pop out.
Dear God, I am thinking it's fun to be me
Seeing your world from the top of a tree.

Thank you, dear God, for our beautiful world,
  And the great wide wonderful sky.
I love looking up when the 'cotton wool' clouds,
Are silently floating by.
And sometimes when you send the sun and the rain
In a shimmering shower together,
A mystical, magical rainbow appears –
How I wish it would stay there forever.

I learned it on the meadow path
  I learned it on the mountain stairs
The best things any mortal hath
Are those which every mortal shares.

Thank you, God, that we all
can share your wonderful love.

God, you've given so much to me
  Sun and sand and sky and sea,
Stars that shine to light the way
And dawn that brings another day.

As each morn comes fresh and new
I will share my thoughts with you
And may I ever mindful be
That God is love, and God loves me.

God our Father of the world, please help us to love one another.
  Make nations friendly with other nations,
Make all of us love one another.
Help us to do our part to bring peace
in the world and happiness to all men.

Prayer from Japan

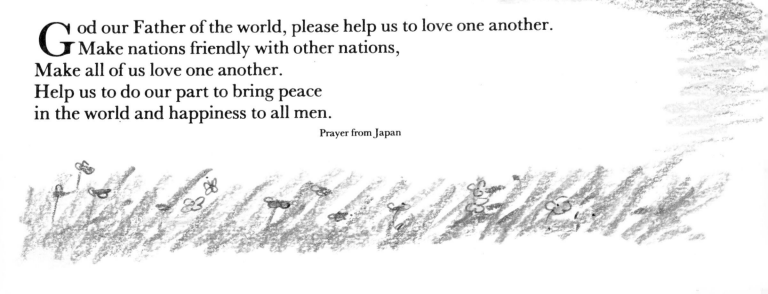

Good night, God!

Lord bless us and keep us and make
Your face to shine upon us.

Numbers 6:25

The day is done
Gone is the sun
Dear Father, bless us every one.

O God, be my guardian
Stay always with me
In the morning
In the evening
By day or by night
Be my helper.

A prayer from Poland

O come to my heart, Lord Jesus,
There is room in my heart for you.

Good night, dear Lord, and may I say,
Thank you for another day.
Keep me safe tonight, I pray,
And eager for tomorrow.
May I grow up kind and caring
Joyfully your blessings sharing.
Following the way you tread
Thank you, Lord, it's time for bed.
Amen.